How to Become

a Spy

*A Guide to Developing
Spy Skills and Joining the
Elite Underworld of Secret
Agents and Spy Operatives*

by Maxwell Knight

Table of Contents

Introduction

While there are many national and international law enforcement agencies, it was decided long ago by the powers-that-be that these agencies weren't entirely adequate to deal with the largest problem in any conflict or its resolution efforts: information!

To deal with that problem, the first intelligence agencies were formed. Over the years, their scope in law enforcement has vastly increased and blurred across many avenues of official intelligence gathering and dissemination, analysis, and counterespionage.

And so the biggest childhood dream of many kids across the globe was born—to become a spy, the elite of the elite!

It's good to note that James Bond and other celluloid spies are about as far removed from reality and rationale as possible, being the biggest bunch of failures to enter the espionage business. No antagonist ever fails to recognize Bond, which goes against the whole essence of spying: avoiding detection to gather information. And if by a small miracle Bond does avoid detection, he then proceeds to introduce himself like a dramatic moron. However, despite Bond's counterintuitive approach to spying, the spies we see on the silver screen still exemplify plenty of basic field skills that a good spy needs to develop.

Before we launch into this guide, there are two things you need to keep in mind. First, becoming a spy isn't a general ambition—it has to become the overriding goal of your life if you ever want to accomplish it. Second, the skills and exercises in this guide are listed with the inherent assumption that they aren't to be misused or utilized to circumvent the law. After all, to be a spy for your country means that you're the first line of defense in the fight of good versus evil!

Are you ready to learn the cool tricks that form the bread and butter of a field operative? Are you ready to learn exactly what path your life needs to take if you wish to become a covert operative? Let's get started!

Chapter 1: The Basic Qualities of a Covert Operative

Quality 1: Intelligence

Since you're going to be an 'intelligence' officer, it's a given that this needs to be one of the most rudimentary qualities of a spy, isn't it? However, intelligence comes in many shapes and forms, and book knowledge is not the only thing that's counted when it comes to being a spy—you need common sense and creative thinking as well.

A spy needs to be able to deal with any situation as it comes, as most of the situations you'll encounter on the job will be unpredictable. Tactical thinking, a masterful memory, a great eye for detail, and a firm grasp of what makes others tick are all must-haves for a successful covert operative. This should be complemented by other intellectual traits, such as being a quick study and having a vast knowledge of matters outside your everyday life. Specialized knowledge, such as detailed technical understanding of chemistry, physics and other related branches of science, is often highly sought-after in field operatives, too. Above all, an intelligence officer must be able to think fast on their feet and formulate creative solutions in dealing with tactical and political issues that they will come across on a daily basis.

Quality 2: Courage

No one says that covert operatives need to be entirely fearless. After all, many great men have said that there is no one less trustworthy than a completely fearless person; such people are either froth-at-the-mouth mad or too stupid to understand the situation. However, due to the nature of their profession, covert operatives have to push past their innate fear every day in order to pursue their line of work, or at least channel that fear to inspire them to come up with better solutions in order to avoid the development of unpredictable situations. This makes courage—and the ability to keep acting with a cool head under stress, pressure, or danger—a must-have.

Quality 3: Physical Fitness

Since this line of work often calls for joint operations with military or law enforcement—and in itself possesses many demands which may be intrinsically physical—fitness is an extremely important attribute for every successful covert operative.

Again, while no one needs you to be built like a mountain—in fact, that might hamper your chances of getting the job—you still need to be far fitter than the average human being. After all, it's much easier to disguise yourself as unfit than it is to tell your body to be fit when you're depending on it in the middle of an operation.

So intelligence, courage, and fitness form the basic qualities of a good intelligence operative. The best part about these qualities is that every single one of these can be learned if you start preparing for them right now. *That* is exactly what the ensuing chapters will be about. This guide will take you through the basic skills needed by a field operative, the many ways to develop these qualities, as well as the academic path and qualifications your life needs to take if you ever wish to become a spy.

I should also point out that if you have ancestry or citizenship from any of the 'hard countries' (nations that are difficult for foreign government personnel or other operatives to enter officially, such as North Korea) or other such nations in active or passive conflict with the erstwhile Allied nations such as the

United States, then you have an advantage in the selection process, since covert agencies are actively recruiting from among these ethnic groups.

Apart from the points mentioned above, here are a few more things which you need to remember if you're ever to become a spy:

[1] Clean Criminal Record – Live a spotless life, and don't get into trouble with the police. If you have any sort of a criminal record, you're likely to be disqualified from the selection process from the get-go.

[2] No Drug Abuse – You're going to be extensively tested for drug abuse when you apply to become a spy. Covert agencies have a zero-tolerance policy on substance abuse and addictions. If you've experimented with illegal drugs in the past, I would strongly recommend you quit now. When applying to become an intelligence operative, you're required to disclose your past history with drugs, if any, and at that point in time, I strongly urge you to tell the truth. One way or the other, it *will* be revealed in your background check, and your honesty may do you credit at that point. If you bring a truckload of valuable skillsets, a history of experimentation with drugs in the past *just* might not weigh against you.

However, if you want the best chance at getting your dream job, I strongly recommend keeping clean altogether.

[3] Excellent Academic Record – Even though academic knowledge is just one of the forms of intelligence treasured by agencies, they *do* want the best of the best. Apart from great physical fitness and athletic abilities, you need to maintain an excellent academic record if you want to join a covert intelligence organization. Many require potential candidates to have a 3.2 GPA and above just to qualify as applicants. Furthermore, depending on the agency you apply to, the qualification requirement varies from a basic bachelor's degree to a full-on doctorate.

[4] Citizenship – You need to be a registered citizen of your nation. Not only that, but your closest family members have to be registered citizens of your nation as well. Even if you're married, your spouse needs to be a registered citizen of the country.

[5] Age – The upper age limit for applicants in most intelligence organizations is 35. As far as the lower age limits are concerned, you can apply to covert agencies while still in high school. The age requirements for each agency are posted on their website.

[6] Low Public Profile – If you want to be effective as a spy, you need to stay away from the limelight. The logic behind this is pretty simple: if you're undercover and someone remembers your real name because they saw your Facebook profile picture or an old photograph online, your mission is blown. The easiest way to avoid this, if you're serious about becoming a spy, is to get off social media sites right away. Remove any profiles you may have on any websites, and remove your picture from any third-party hosting sites. Google yourself to check where you may pop up, and send emails to the relevant sites to have your photo removed. Of course, don't tell them it's because you want to be a spy!

[7] Keep Your Ambitions to Yourself – If you announce your dreams to your friends and family, you're unlikely to ever become a covert operative even if you manage to get recruited into agencies like the CIA. Share your ambitions only with your immediate family, and even then, tell them only with the reminder that they should keep this information to themselves.

Chapter 2: Physical Training to Become a Spy

Before we get to the fun part about field skills, let's discuss the many ways of attaining the basic qualities we've gone through in the previous chapter. After all, if you don't intend to follow these basics, then you'll never be selected as a spy, regardless of how well you can shadow someone.

If you intend to remain a couch potato for the rest of your life, merely dreaming of spy operations in casinos in Monaco with beautiful women draped on your arms, then that's exactly where your chances of becoming a spy will remain—in your dreams.

Covert agencies have a marked preference for ex-military personnel for three major reasons: they're disciplined in action and thought; they are physically fit and usually remain so for the greater part of their lives; and they have been fiercely trained in various forms of combat.

If you wish to train yourself to be a spy, yet have no desire to join the military, then your best bet is to get in great shape through self-defense and other hand-to-hand combat training.

Since it's unlikely you'll be tasked to go undercover as an Olympic weight-lifter, and it's been already mentioned that being built like a house would probably hamper your chances, it's best to get started on rigorous cardiovascular training. Join a gym or start exercising on your own, whichever will be more effective for you. Hit the treadmill or get into jogging. Work on developing leaner muscles, which are better suited for repetitive exercise, greater strain, and a physically active lifestyle while maintaining flexibility, rather than the puffed-up muscles of weight junkies.

You should also work on breathing exercises through meditative techniques. This is done to develop more control over your breathing rate and the sounds of your breath, which will be invaluable if you're shadowing someone.

On top of getting in shape through cardiovascular routines and other exercises such as crunches, pull-ups, and push-ups, get yourself into a few self-defense classes and work hard to master them. The most suitable combat disciplines for active use in any sort of situation are usually Muay Thai and other forms of kickboxing like Aikido and Jiujitsu. The martial art forms which were specifically formulated or developed for military use, such as Krav Maga and Combat Sambo, are also great options.

For free-form movement and great physical development, you can learn and practice parkour as well. Apart from requiring high levels of fitness, the movement styles in parkour are regularly used by operatives in real environments out on the streets.

Remember that the point of learning these techniques is not to become a street bully, nor are they merely for show. Someday, your life will truly be in peril and what you learn here can save your life. You need to pursue this with the dedication and seriousness required to become a master practitioner.

Also, your military competitors during the selection process will have learned martial arts forms relevant to combat situations, and will have actively honed their skills in their field of work. Will you be able to say the same by that point?

Chapter 3: Mental Training to Become a Spy

Although the academic requirements to become a spy are quite high, that isn't the sort of training I intend to address in this section—though what you do here will help tremendously with your studies as well.

Free app stores are a boon to modern civilization, and there are apps present to suit all needs. Find and concentrate on games which help improve reflexes and memory. Reflexes depend on the speed with which your neurons fire impulses, as well as the speed with which your muscles respond to those impulses. Memory, on the other hand, depends on attention and the effectiveness of your short-term and long-term memory storage. Both of these attributes can, to a very large extent, be trained. Search and download the most interesting reflex and memory games for yourself, and spend at least half an hour on them every day.

Nowadays, covert agencies don't hire operatives unless they're multilingual, so you need to start learning a few secondary languages. At the very least, you should be fluent in one or two languages other than your native tongue. However, it's not enough just to learn them: you need to be thoroughly fluent in them, and also work to eradicate any traces of a foreign accent. The best part about this is that it's easily achievable through language apps available online. You can learn and practice any number of languages and teach yourself to become as fluent in them as possible, all on your own. Keep in mind though that some languages are given more importance than others. For example, it's far more valuable to be able to fluently speak and write in Farsi, Arabic, Mandarin, Cantonese, or Korean than in French or German.

In addition, you should also study the native culture behind each language you learn in order to give you an edge over other competitors. This will make it far easier to understand *how* the native people use their language, rather than just understanding what they're saying. Idioms and phrases, for example, are heavily culture-dependent and form a regular part of speech among native speakers. Kudos if you're also able to learn the dialects of your chosen language.

Aside from reflex and memory games and secondary languages, you should also start practicing codes for fun. As an example, if you write in a diary, devise a code that only you can understand and use it to encrypt the information you put in your diary. Not only will you have a lot of fun coming up with your own codes, it'll work better than any lock or mattress to safeguard your diary from siblings, parents and nosy roommates. You can also strike a deal with your parents or partner to write the shopping lists for you in code. If you can't crack the code in a set time, they'll have to tell you the solution in return for you doing 'xyz' chores. If you manage to break the code, then you can ask for a small reward of your choosing, like more pocket money or fewer chores. An understanding of cryptography, and a mind that's well-honed to cracking different kinds of codes, is extremely valuable to intelligence organizations, so follow this recommendation seriously.

There are also several certified organizations in most major cities which provide hacking and counter-hacking certifications and classes. Join one of these classes and study hard to gain counter-hacking skills. It's rather obvious why this should be a valuable resource for a spy. Additionally, some of these organizations are affiliated with certain departments and branches of intelligence agencies and, as such, could offer chances for employment—or at least recommendations for your application which would give you a great edge when you apply for recruitment and selection.

Chapter 4: Basic Field Skills to Be a Spy

Now comes the part each of you are eagerly waiting for, and don't bother denying it. This is by far the most fun part of practicing to become a spy.

Skill 1: Blending Into a Crowd

Out of all the survival skills you need to become a spy, this one is by far the most important. While your physical training should adequately equip you with almost every skill you need to survive conflict, your chances of living through your job are always higher if you avoid conflict to begin with.

The first thing you need to get out of your head is this worldwide fascination with the color black when it comes to spying. No color scheme is more suspicious or attention grabbing than all black—except maybe someone in Joey Buttafuoco pants and a Dr. Seuss hat. Grey is the real color of invisibility. So if you want to successfully blend into a crowd, wear muted colors, preferably shades of grey. Also, don't think that covering your head would make you less noticeable. Someone hiding under a hood is about as invisible as an ostrich with its head buried in the sand.

23

While the actual apparel that you wear depends on the crowd you're trying to blend into, this color scheme rule never changes. Also, avoid anything shiny or reflective, including sunglasses. You'll blend in far more easily with fake spectacles instead.

The best way to blend into a crowd is to stay in the open and pretend you belong there. Don't ever run or rush, just calmly walk through the crowd with your shoulders slightly hunched forward and your head angled slightly downward. If you're too tall to successfully blend into a crowd, avoid any footwear that adds to your height and slightly bend your knees while you walk. Between the bent knees and the hunched shoulders and back, you'd be surprised by how much shorter a tall person can appear. This tip will serve you well regardless of the clothes you're wearing or the crowd with which you're trying to blend into.

To practice this technique, plan to meet with friends at a busy or crowded spot. Put on grey clothes that would blend in well with the agreed upon location and wait for medium to large crowds to walk around the spot where your friends are waiting. Try to blend into the crowd as best you can, and walk a few circles around your friends without them noticing you before finally approaching them. While this may not be a success from the get-go, you'll learn from your mistakes fast enough and should be able to accomplish this after a few attempts.

You should also use this exercise to think of ways in which your target could have figured you out, and use that to develop habits to avoid a tail if you were the intended target. This should reveal the small, unconscious habits that most people don't realize they have—and which make it easy to follow them. It will also help you improve your own tailing, much like a star quarterback watching his game footage to improve his skills on the field.

Skill 2 – How to Shadow or 'Tail' Someone

Note: Do not use this to become a creepy stalker!

The main thing to remember is that human minds are sensitive to repetitive coincidences. If the person you're shadowing knows you and sees you around them more than once, they're going to get their guard up which will make your job much more difficult.

Always keep a pace of at least thirty feet between you and the person you're shadowing. Keep one or two groups of people between the two of you at all times. Don't always walk behind them—instead cross the street, turn your back and use the reflections from shop fronts to keep an eye on your target. If they're taking a turn and dropping out of sight, don't rush forward or run just to catch up. Leave the same distance as before and keep calmly walking onward. Chances are they'll still be on the same path anyway, and you won't look as suspicious to others around you (who might find it odd to see someone running up just to take a glance down a road).

When following someone at night or in a secluded area, match your movements with the natural sounds of the area. Always stick to the darkest shadows and don't rush forward even if you think you may lose your target. It's better to lose your target now and try again tomorrow than get caught. Remember that if you're searching in shadows under trees, you need to pay attention to where you step and avoid fallen leaves and branches to avoid making unnecessary noises. In dark areas, you need to remember that humans have a halfway decent night vision which kicks in after some time spent free from exposure to lights. So if you're tailing someone in a dark area, you may want to hide behind objects and move from hiding spot to hiding spot instead of just walking in the darkest shadows.

Whenever you're picking a shadow, you should also choose ones that are immediately around or behind powerful lights. This is because lights lower your target's visual sensitivity to darkness, which will make it even more difficult to pick you out.

Also, if you're waiting to tail someone, or your target gets suspicious after they happen to notice you, carrying a book or a newspaper is supremely pointless. Instead, plug your earphones into your smartphone and keep a game switched on, or some music playing. It's important to have something you may have actively been doing on the screen since a blank screen is just as suspicious.

If your target has spotted you, it's also best to walk up to him or her yourself and pretend to be the one surprised to see them rather than acting as though you didn't notice (or weren't following) that person.

If you're following someone in a vehicle, keep in mind that vehicles are far easier to spot and remember than a person tailing on foot. This is the main reason why tailing with vehicles is performed by teams and not by a singular personnel during operations; the team that started the tail on the target is switched out by another at regular intervals through a journey.

If you're following someone by car or bike, always keep at least three vehicles between you and your target. In that manner, you can keep an eye on your target's vehicle while using the vehicles in between to hide from their sight.

There are a number of ways to practice these techniques. If you have siblings who are aware of your ambitions, set up bets and challenges. Inform them that you could be following them at any time of the day, and place a bet on whether they can notice you or not. If they're meeting up with friends in crowded places, follow them through their evening for an hour or two before returning home. Take pictures with your cell phone for evidence. This will also allow you to practice gathering visual intelligence without getting caught. You can also practice the first skill (blending into a crowd) by attempting to get closer to them while tailing to see how effectively you can blend and escape notice from a target who is extremely familiar with you. In such a case, changing the way you walk helps escape notice too, since a person's gait is usually quite distinct.

Skill 3 – Lip Reading

While this isn't a common skillset for field operatives, it is nonetheless an extremely useful one to have.

Lip reading allows you to understand a conversation from a distance without the need for any gadgetry to transmit audio back to you. Even if you did have the tech available, there may still be times when electronics fail.

You can practice this by using any of your favorite movies which you may have seen countless times and from which you have memorized some of the dialogue. Put the movie on mute, and learn the shape and movement of a mouth when it forms words. Mouth the dialogues along with the movie and shape your mouth according to the actor on screen. This should give you some reasonable practice with the basics of lip reading. Once you feel you're performing reasonably well, switch to a movie you haven't seen before and play it on mute. Try to read the lips of the actors, then rewind and play it with sound to see how well you've performed.

Skill 4 – Planting Objects and Obtaining Evidence without Detection

The ability to place and retrieve a target's possessions without being caught is a pretty fundamental ability which will dictate how well you could gather evidence or plant electronic bugs.

For starters, if your parents know of your ambitions, you can use their help to practice this skill. Tear a page of paper into eight small pieces. Write on each piece, "If you find this, please return it to me, [name]". Now take eight small pen caps, just the caps, and stuff the pieces of paper into them so that only a small corner is sticking out.

Now comes the hard part. Identify eight things that your parents use extensively every day. like laptop bags, closets, etc. Think about places or things they don't allow you to access, or assume that you don't touch anyway. Think of spots within each of these items where you could hide a pen cap where it would go unnoticed. You get higher marks if you choose an object that's almost always with them when they leave home. Now, without being detected or seen by them, hide the pen caps in your identified places. Wait for at least two days for them to notice it. If two days pass, and the caps haven't been found, then you're doing reasonably well. Now, you need to get into those eight articles again and retrieve each of those pieces.

If you managed to get through these two days without a single one of your pen caps being found and returned to you, then it's reasonable to assume that you can up the ante and take a greater risk next time. Choose eight objects again, this time selecting items that are almost always with them, and try to identify spots that humans don't usually pay attention to, like the joint between the heel and the sole in a shoe, and attach your pen caps there. Monitor if the objects are found for another two days.

In this case, if not a single object is found then you probably need better targets to practice on, because either your targets are extremely attention deficient or are humoring you since they know about your dreams.

If you have relatives with a sense of humor and who are close to you, try doing the same in their house the next time you visit them, but maintain some boundaries, i.e. don't break into their wardrobes or medicine cabinets. If they find the pen cap and call you back, take note of the number of days it took them to find it—this should tell you how good of a job you did.

31

With this exercise, you should not only be able to take advantage of your target's time in the bathroom or lack of attention to their possessions, but you should also be able to figure out where someone might hide a bug in your own bedroom. Develop a habit of identifying and checking such suspicious places whenever you stay in a room, whether at someone's home, a dorm room, or in a hotel.

Also, you should use this exercise to develop booby traps, and I don't mean go full-blown *Home Alone* on anyone who enters your room. Just develop systems to tell you if someone's been inside the room or not. If you're reasonably sure no one enters your room while you're gone, you can use the 'hair in the door' trick. Take a strand of hair from a hairbrush or comb (nobody wants to pluck hair from their head everyday), and jam it in the door at head height when you close it. This way, you'll know someone entered the room while you're gone as the hair will have fallen off. It's simple yet effective. If you don't want to do this with a piece of hair, you can do the same with a tiny piece of paper in the crack of the door *along the side with the hinges*. However, this will seem suspicious to an intruder if seen.

Skill 5 – Lie Detection

Learning this skill will ask you to do things that might make you feel a bit foolish, but it pays off big-time in the long run.

Go to your parents or siblings first—one by one, and only if they all know about your dreams—and tell them you're the greatest lie detector on Earth. When they scoff in disbelief, which they should and will, challenge them to tell you three truths and two lies about themselves and that you'll identify the lies once they're done. When they start telling you, pay attention to their eyes, words, and body language. Every human has a different set of tics which shows that they're lying. Some go into unnecessary detail, some scratch the bridge of their nose or eyes or the back of their arms or hands, some clear their throats or pull on their ears, while others blink too often or shuffle their feet unnecessarily. The point is that a lie is usually accompanied by some unnecessary action, and sometimes that action is repeated through every lie.

Unless you're extremely lucky or extremely talented, you're not going to be able to identify the lies from the get-go. Ask them to give you another chance and another set of five. Keep at it till you've gotten some idea of their nervous tic while lying, and hit them with the truth.

Once you're able to identify the tics of one person, move on to the next. Go through your family in the same manner until you've gotten the hang of identifying signs of lying. Then you can move on to challenging your friends in the same way. By this time you should be good enough at identifying a lie to be able to win at least half the challenges with your friends.

You should know that each of these skills have about a hundred different tips and tricks which will make them easier and faster to perform. However, most of these tips depend on your physique and the way your mind absorbs information, and so can only be obtained through *experience*. Basically, the more you challenge yourself in each of these exercises, the better you'll perform when it actually counts and your life is on the line.

While there are several uses of gadgetry in espionage as well, these basic skills are what you'll need to *plant* or *use* that gadgetry to begin with. After all, sitting in a van and listening to people talk through headphones isn't really the difficult part, is it?

Chapter 5: Getting Hired by an Intelligence Agency

We've gone through the major requirements which you'll need to fulfill if you wish to become a covert operative, as well as the various skillsets which would offer you a tremendous advantage over other candidates.

What you need to remember is that you won't be an "agent" in the way that term is used in movies. Essentially, all trained covert operatives are charged with setting up an intelligence network in the region where they're based. That means that if you're transferred to a foreign nation, you're most likely going to be responsible for scouting and recruiting high-value assets. These are people in positions of importance who may have access to valuable information or who may be useful as affiliations through the power of their positions. You will also be in charge of handling their operations, gathering intelligence, and safely transmitting said intel back to headquarters for analysis. Thus, you'll be a case handler or a case officer and *they* will be your agents.

Like earlier mentioned, every agency has their own set of requirements for recruitment, all of which are listed on the websites below (for US citizens):

Central Intelligence Agency -
www.cia.gov/careers/opportunities

National Security Agency -
www.nsa.gov/careers/

For those of you who aren't U.S citizens, most major
intelligence organizations have their own websites
wherein the same details are posted along with
qualifications and methods for application, except for
some that only offer recruitment through invitation or
headhunting from their end.

For U.S citizens, both the NSA and CIA provide
internship opportunities as well as scholarships for
graduate and post-graduate courses in return for a
promise of employment within their organization
upon successful completion of studies.

It's also important to remember that the clandestine
unit (like the Directorate of Operations or the
National Clandestine Service at CIA) only accounts
for 5-10% of the total personnel who are employed
by these agencies.

Even if you are inclined to other careers or aspire to be a physicist, engineer, psychiatrist, doctor, or IT specialist, you can still have a place in these agencies. Many in these professions are vital to the intelligence gathering which forms your nation's first line of defense. They have a long list of career opportunities suited to a wide variety of professions, all of which are mentioned in detail on the websites listed above.

However, as brought up before, these agencies are the cream of the elite and so only hire the best of the best. You need to check the requirements for application and orient yourself right away toward the kind of lifestyle that would best increase your chances of success.

Conclusion

A spy, contrary to what television and movies show us, doesn't get paid a lot. Especially when you consider the real and present danger attached to the job profile. However, these operatives perform their duty to their country out of that most noble of motives: patriotism. It is the intelligence gathered by these self-sacrificing men and women which allows your nation to stay one step ahead of those who wish harm upon it. It is this same intelligence force which allows your nation to respond to an attack quickly and efficiently, or bring to justice those who have wronged its citizens.

Since you wish to count yourself a part of this elite group, you need to give the profession its due respect and look at it as more than cool toys and a crazy, jet-setting life. You need to remember that while your rose-tinted vision may paint a mysterious and appealing life right now, being a spy has just as many downsides as perks. You will never be able to tell your friends or family what you really do for a living. You will never be the celebrated hero, rather always the unsung protector in the shadows watching over those who need the sacrifice of you and your colleagues.

All the risks notwithstanding, the life of a spy presents a worthy cause for sacrifice, and if you're ready to bear that cross, then you need to start making the effort to gear yourself toward that path right away!

Finally, I'd like to thank you for purchasing this book! If you enjoyed it or found it helpful, I'd greatly appreciate it if you'd take a moment to leave a review on Amazon. Thank you!

Made in the USA
Columbia, SC
13 September 2020